To:

....

From:

....

Date:

....

GodMoments
for
You

Carolyn Larsen

christian art gifts®

GodMoments for You

Copyright © 2012 Carolyn Larsen
All rights reserved.

Developed in co-operation with Educational Publishing
Concepts

© 2012 Christian Art Gifts, RSA
        Christian Art Gifts Inc., IL, USA

Designed by Christian Art Gifts

Images used under license from Shutterstock.com

Scripture quotations are taken from the *Holy Bible*, New
International Version® NIV®. Copyright © 1973, 1978, 1984,
2011 by International Bible Society. Used by permission of
Zondervan Publishing House. All rights reserved.

Printed in China

ISBN 978-1-77036-903-0

12 13 14 15 16 17 18 19 20 21 – 12 11 10 9 8 7 6 5 4 3

Introduction

Hey there,

I can just hear what you are thinking ... "My life is CRAZY busy. I cannot ... simply cannot add one more thing to my schedule. Sure, I want to spend time with God ... but WHEN?"

Yes, I hear you and I'm right there with you. We seem to live our lives on the proverbial hamster wheel and we make choices every day as to what we have time for and what we have to let go. But, the truth is that starting your day by spending a moment with God (if you only have a moment) will definitely make your day better. So, take a few moments to focus your heart on the truth of His presence with you in every circumstance.

Allow His love to guide you through this busy day in all you do and in all your relationships.

A God Moment makes a God Day!

Words of Wisdom

*May these words of my mouth and this
meditation of my heart be pleasing in Your
sight, Lord, my Rock and my Redeemer.*
- Psalm 19:14 -

Words come flying out of the mouth so easily sometimes, don't they? If you've had a bad day at work, words of anger shoot out at anyone who gets in the way. If you're discouraged or depressed or just don't really like another person – watch out!

Of course you make excuses, apologize and hope for forgiveness. But the truth is angry, unkind words lay on a person's heart for a long time. Words that are unkind, angry, attacking or just plain old mean, do not in any way show the light of Christ. In fact, they are just the opposite. They can damage your own witness and if spouted at unbelievers can push them farther away from Christ.

Ask God to help you hold your tongue and remember that your words reflect Him to others.

*Words which do not give the light
of Christ, increase the darkness.*
- Mother Teresa -

Honest Worship

Great is the Lord and most
worthy of praise; His greatness
no one can fathom.
- Psalm 145:3 -

God is. That's the bottom line. Just because a person refuses to believe doesn't make God any less real.

But, let's talk about believers ... like you. You've accepted Christ. You pray, read your Bible and worship. Until you get mad at God. Yeah, you've prayed about something for a while – the need for a job or healing for a sick loved one or some other major thing and God doesn't do what you think He should. So, you refuse to worship or maybe your heart is too bruised to worship.

Don't worry, God can handle your honesty. He knows you're hurting and He cares. He is still God and He will wait until your heart can worship again. You are not diminishing His glory, you are working through a new depth of relationship with Him.

A man can no more diminish God's glory
by refusing to worship Him than a lunatic
can put out the sun by scribbling the word,
"darkness" on the walls of his cell.
- C.S. Lewis -

Healing Forgiveness

"And forgive us our debts,
as we also have forgiven our debtors."
- Matthew 6:12 -

A friend ... or at least someone you thought was a friend has spread some nasty rumors about you. Anger races through your heart ... you want to hurt right back ... get even. Is that right?

Well, it's a natural response to hurt. Hopefully you don't act on that natural response, especially since God encourages His followers to forgive and show love ... even to enemies. No, it isn't easy, but think about the possibilities of what the response to forgiveness can be.

Forgiving someone who hurts you is an overt act of love toward that person. It is an opportunity to obviously show the love of God and what a pleasant impact that can have on another person. Hopefully it will be the beginning of healing.

Forgiveness is the fragrance the violet
sheds on the heel that has crushed it.
- Mark Twain -

Beauty Is in the Eye of the Beholder

The Lord said to Samuel,
"Do not consider his appearance
or his height, for I have rejected him.
The Lord does not look at the things
people look at. People look at the outward
appearance, but the Lord looks at the heart."
- 1 Samuel 16:7 -

Beauty is a hot topic in the world today. A lot of time and money is spent in the pursuit of beauty. Women want to look beautiful and to be considered beautiful by the men in their lives. Men want a beautiful woman on their arm.

But, what is beauty? Is it a classic face? Is it a movie star figure? Is it an expensive haircut or designer clothes? It really is none of those things.

True beauty comes from within. It begins in the heart that reflects the love, compassion and gentleness of God. So, while the world may bombard us with one definition of beauty, God's definition is focused completely on something else. It focuses on the heart that considers others and serves them as it serves and obeys God. What a beautiful spirit!

God's definition of beauty is a lot different than
the world's. God says that beauty is found
in a gentle, quiet, obedient spirit.
- Heather Whitestone -

A Life of Faith

For we live by faith, not by sight.
- 2 Corinthians 5:7 -

It would be nice to have a script for your whole life, wouldn't it? You'd know everything that was coming – every crisis, every change, every joy and every sorrow. There would be no surprises.

Actually, it would not be a good thing because you would know everything that was coming and sometimes you would want to run! Living by faith means that you trust God and you know He has a plan for your life and that He is working out that plan in His own good time.

So, even when something happens that you don't understand, you don't have to be afraid. You can trust that every crisis and every situation is leading you to the next thing that God has for you.

A life of faith means trusting in God no matter what happens – even when YOU don't know where it's leading. You can trust in the truth that God knows!

Faith is taking the first step even when you don't see the whole staircase.
- Martin Luther King, Jr -

Take a Step

"So do not fear, for I am with you;
do not be dismayed, for I am your God.
I will strengthen you and help you;
I will uphold you with My righteous right hand."
- Isaiah 41:10 -

Think of the heroes of the Bible – Moses, Noah, Esther. None of these men or women were superheroes, but their lives are considered great by those who read of them today.

The key to the success of the people of Scripture and the people of history is that they took the first step. God asked things of them and they obeyed. Moses didn't know where his first step was going to lead. Esther had no idea she would be used to save her people when she entered the beauty contest. None of their greatness would have happened if they had not taken the first step.

What is God asking of you? Is there something you know God is asking of you but you haven't yet started? Get busy – you never know where it's going to lead you!

You don't have to be great to start
but you have to start to be great.
- Zig Ziglar -

The Happiness Choice

"I know the plans I have for you,"
declares the Lord, "plans to prosper
you and not to harm you, plans to
give you hope and a future."
- Jeremiah 29:11 -

Happiness is a fleeting emotion and emotions are roller coasters that fluctuate with changing circumstances.

One constant of life is change, so it is a choice to accept change with a cheerful attitude. That can't happen unless you are convinced that none of the changes in your life have surprised God. Believing that He is in control gives you the confidence to choose a positive attitude toward whatever happens.

So, happiness is a choice that is founded in trusting God. Has the history of your walk with God given you the confidence needed to choose happiness? If not, take that first step and choose a cheerful attitude based on the knowledge that God is in control!

I have also learned from experience that the greater
part of our happiness or misery depends upon our
dispositions, and not upon our circumstances.
- Martha Washington -

God's Deep Love

*I am convinced that neither death nor life,
neither angels nor demons, neither the
present nor the future, nor any powers,
neither height nor depth, nor anything
else in all creation, will be able to
separate us from the love of God
that is in Christ Jesus our Lord.*
- Romans 8:38-39 -

"It feels like my pilot light has gone out," a friend confessed to me. She looked like that, too ... tired, unenthusiastic about life, just completely worn out.

Life had taken a few left turns for her leaving her with a broken marriage, working in a job she didn't enjoy, having to let go of a particular ministry that gave great fulfillment. All of these changes took the enthusiasm out of her life. She had even lost the sense of her connection with God.

So, we talked about God and how much He loves her. I committed to pray for her every day and she committed to a daily time with God – even if it was short – to reconnect with Him and let Him relight that pilot light.

*Nobody grows old merely by living a number
of years. We grow old by deserting our ideals.
Years may wrinkle the skin, but to give
up enthusiasm wrinkles the soul.*
- Samuel Ullman -

The Little Things

You go to a drive-through restaurant and once you're back on the road you discover you've been given too much change. Way too much. Or, figuring your income tax is done at the very last possible minute and later you discover you've forgotten something important ... that would mean you owe more.

Or, in the rush of life you speak very curtly to your spouse or friend. Any one of these circumstances could be considered a little thing but any one of them can lead to bigger problems.

Pay attention to the little things because they are what make up a life. Little things can wreck a life or can present individual opportunities to live for God and allow Him to shine through you in the practical aspects of your everyday life.

*Watch the little things; a small
leak will sink a great ship.*
- Benjamin Franklin -

Self-Importance

*"Therefore, whoever takes the lowly
position of this child is the greatest
in the kingdom of heaven."*
- Matthew 18:4 -

Honesty time ... do you know a person who is often quite vocal and opinionated ... so much so that when you see him or her coming you run the other way?

Some people seem to have no filter as to when to stop talking and don't even realize that they are not really saying anything. It's actually a form of pride to feel so self-important that you think your opinion and your ideas are always more important than anyone else's.

In relationships, it is important to be able to listen and give someone else the chance to be heard. You can be a God moment for someone else as you stand back in humility and allow someone else to shine.

*Wise men speak because they have something to say,
fools because they have to say something.*
- Plato -

The Privilege of Prayer

The Lord is near to all who call on Him,
to all who call on Him in truth.
- Psalm 145:18 -

A personal relationship with God means you are able to talk with Him ... as you are able to talk with a loved one.

You can spill the concerns of your heart. You can bring the needs of your friends and family to Him. You can ask His help with whatever you are facing in life. Through this privilege of prayer your relationship with God will deepen. You will get to know Him better. You will get to know yourself better. So why do we not pray more often? Why do we take this privilege so lightly? Why does it sometimes become a chore that we must attend to rather than a joy?

Coming to God and first confessing sin and asking forgiveness presents a clean heart to talk about whatever concerns you. Don't neglect this privilege and the relationship building it affords to you!

Prayer should not be regarded as a duty
which must be performed, but rather as a
privilege to be enjoyed, a rare delight that
is always revealing some new beauty.
- E. M. Bounds -

Love, Don't Judge

*"A new command I give you:
Love one another. As I have loved you,
so you must love one another."*
- John 13:34 -

God put a lot of emphasis on love. So, why is it so hard for us to just love others sometimes?

Against God's wishes, we build these imaginary boxes that we want others to fit into. If people don't live by the rules we find acceptable, then we judge them as failures and we either disassociate with them or try to change them to be what we want. In all that work the love gets lost.

Think about how Jesus accepted people. He loved people who were not really very loveable. He loved people that the religious leaders condemned. He loves you, even with all your foibles.

Can we follow His example? How will we influence people to come to know Christ and love Him if we can't love them?

*If you judge people,
you do not have time to love them.*
- Mother Teresa -

Go for the Cure

Therefore do not let sin reign in your mortal body so that you obey its evil desires. Do not offer any part of yourself to sin as an instrument of wickedness, but rather offer yourselves to God as those who have been brought from death to life; and offer every part of yourself to Him as an instrument of righteousness.
- Romans 6:12-13 -

Sure you want to get rid of sin in your life, who wouldn't? You probably especially want to get rid of those sinful habits that haunt you day after day. You've prayed and asked God to help you overcome those sins but still have a daily struggle with them.

That's because you have to do your part to get rid of sin. There is no easy way out. It doesn't work to pray about it, but then go right on giving in to it every time you're tempted. If you don't really, truly want that sin out of your life, then it isn't going anywhere.

Don't settle for a cover-up, do your part to get rid of the sin! Even if it takes hard work, go for the cure!

You would think that everyone would leap at the chance to get rid of sin. Not so. They want relief not a cure.
- Dr. Henry Brandt -

Building Bridges

*"For in the same way you judge others,
you will be judged, and with the measure
you use, it will be measured to you."*
- Matthew 7:2 -

You and your spouse have been best friends with another couple for years and years. Suddenly (well, suddenly to you) your best friend goes off the deep end ... drugs, alcohol, he or she even has an affair and ends up divorced. This leaves you feeling hurt, angry and confused about your friendship.

Do you cut this person out of your life and stay close with the spouse who was dumped? Do you preach to this friend about broken spiritual laws and broken vows? Do you just cast him or her off to the evil of this sin and walk away?

Think about what Jesus would do. He worked with people who were known sinners because if He had nothing to do with them, how would they get to know Him? Same for you – your mercy to another person may be the bridge that brings him or her back to Christ. Think about your responsibility, not about your judgment of another.

*I have always found that mercy bears
richer fruits than strict justice.*
- Abraham Lincoln -

Take a Stand

Before a word is on my tongue, You, Lord,
know it completely. You hem me in behind
and before, and You lay Your hand upon me.
- Psalm 139:4-5 -

Taking a stand on something can be scary. Once you state your beliefs you will, no doubt, find people who disagree with you. Some will disagree loudly and angrily. Friends may begin to take a step back when you approach, for fear of being associated with you.

So, what's the option? Keep your opinions to yourself? Turn away from injustices and just let them happen? Hide your head in the sand? Is that what God wants you to do? How will horrible situations around the world be changed if no one speaks up? How will people even come to know Christ if His followers are silent?

Taking a stand can mean taking a risk, but you never stand alone. Even if friends and family step away – God is always beside you … in front of you … behind you. He is always with you.

Our lives begin to end the day we
become silent about things that matter.
- Martin Luther King, Jr -

Be Kind

Anyone who withholds kindness from a
friend forsakes the fear of the Almighty.
- Job 6:14 -

Some days it seems like all the crazies in the world are having a convention where you are, doesn't it? You know what I'm talking about. Some days it feels like you are surrounded by drivers that haven't been behind the wheel in years, or restaurant waitrons who took a cranky pill before coming to work, or store clerks who can't answer a question in a civil voice.

Sometimes the crazies are friends or family members who are just hard to get along with on a given day. Today's quote is a good reminder that those "crazies" might not be crazies at all – but instead are probably normal people who are dealing with heavy loads of bad news, oppressive bosses, unhappy home situations, health issues ... the list goes on and on.

Everyone is dealing with something. Take the opportunity to put a smile on your face and a kind word in your mouth and actually BE the love of God to someone who needs it more than you know.

Be kinder than necessary, for everyone you
meet is fighting some kind of battle.
- Anonymous -

Share Courage

*Because of the service by which you
have proved yourselves, others will praise
God for the obedience that accompanies
your confession of the gospel of Christ,
and for your generosity in sharing
with them and with everyone else.*
- 2 Corinthians 9:13 -

One thing I love about autumn is fresh picked juicy apples. Yum, I can almost taste that sweet, juicy fresh fruit.

Sometimes my family goes to a local orchard and buys a basket of fresh apples. It's such a disappointment to pull out the first apple and see one underneath that has begun to rot because that rottenness spreads so quickly to the other apples around it. If the rotten one isn't pulled out, it quickly ruins the entire basket of fruit.

You know, people can do that to each other, too. A bad attitude or even an unreasonable fear can be spread to other people and ruin their outlook on life. On the flip side, a positive attitude of courage and trust in God can also be shared with others, encouraging them to trust God more with their lives.

*Keep your fears to yourself,
but share your courage with others.*
- Robert Louis Stevenson -

Fly High

*But be very careful to keep the
commandment and the law that
Moses the servant of the Lord gave you:
to love the Lord your God, to walk in
obedience to Him, to keep His commands,
to hold fast to Him and to serve Him
with all your heart and with all your soul.*
- Joshua 22:5 -

My daughter wants to fly. I don't mean that she wants to pilot an airplane. I mean she has these dreams of doing amazing things in ministry.

She wants to go to other countries – some that are kind of dangerous places. I wouldn't get to see her for long, long periods of time. My instinct is to hold her back, keep her close to home so I can see her often and know that she is safe.

But, deep in my heart I know that would be wrong. She wouldn't be happy with me. God wouldn't be happy with me because He has planted this calling in her heart. I wouldn't even be happy with me because I would know I am making the two of them unhappy. So, I need to let her fly ... of course, I will be praying like crazy for her. But ... that's a good thing.

*One can never consent to creep when
one feels an impulse to soar.*
- Helen Keller -

Sound Advice

*We, however, will not boast beyond proper
limits, but will confine our boasting to the
sphere of service God Himself has assigned
to us, a sphere that also includes you.*
- 2 Corinthians 10:13 -

People who feel that they have the right to
spout their opinions on everything make me crazy!
This type of person feels the need to "advise"
parents on how to parent, married couples on how
to be married, workers ... virtually any opinion
that comes to their minds comes out their mouths.

Interestingly, these people are sometimes the
least involved in actually doing things. The lesson
here is that if you have an opinion it is a good idea to
precede it with experience. Before you tell someone
how to do something, try it yourself. Others will
be much more apt to listen to you if you actually
know what you're talking about.

Living for God is all about relationships,
building them and strengthening them as we
encourage and help one another. So ... do before
speaking!

*A man of words and not of deeds
is like a garden full of weeds.*
- Anonymous -

God Moments

"And surely I am with you always,
to the very end of the age."
- Matthew 28:20 -

I just heard someone say it again last night, "I had a God Moment today." What is a God Moment? You've probably had them, even if you didn't call them that. A God Moment is that instant in your day when you are aware that God is involved in your life – actively, purposefully and constantly. It's when something happens that you know happened only because of Him.

What a joy to be reminded that God is in everything. Sometimes the problems of life weigh us down and we can lose the awareness that He is constantly watching over us and loving us.

The God Moments are precious reminders that He is paying attention, loving us, directing our lives and protecting us. So when you are blessed with a God Moment, thank Him and remember that it's just one awareness of the thousands of things He does for you every day.

If you live close to God and His infinite grace,
you don't have to tell; it shows on your face.
- Anonymous -

Love the One You're With

Be devoted to one another in love.
Honor one another above yourselves.
- Romans 12:10 -

Do you know what a scattered mind is like? It's when you've got so many things on your mind that you can't focus on one single thing.

While you're doing one thing, you're thinking about something else so you're never fully in the moment. You miss a lot of enjoyment when you live like that. You also miss a lot of the people you are around. If you're not fully engaged in the experiences and conversations you have, you will miss a lot of the emotions and feelings that people try to share with you.

A big part of loving others is sharing with them, listening to them and giving them the gift of your total presence. It's difficult to minister to others without being present with them. How can God work through you to a person if you aren't completely present? Yes, life is busy, but don't let it get so busy that you are not fully where you should be!

Wherever you are, be all there.
- Jim Elliot -

Problem or Opportunity?

*Not only so, but we also glory in our sufferings,
because we know that suffering produces
perseverance; perseverance, character;
and character, hope. And hope does not
put us to shame, because God's love has
been poured out into our hearts through
the Holy Spirit, who has been given to us.*
- Romans 5:3-5 -

Do the problems you face in life make you stronger? Or, do they make you discouraged, hopeless or angry? God doesn't allow problems in our lives simply to be roadblocks or speed bumps. He loves us, so why would He do that?

Have you ever watched a tree bent nearly double by the wind and wonder what kept it from snapping in two? The very wind that is testing it is what made it strong and flexible. In the same way, problems keep us coming to God, trusting Him, asking for His help and guidance. Problems give us the experience of seeing God come through. With each problem, we learn we can trust Him more. A pretty cool way to think about problems, eh?

*Good timber does not grow with ease.
The stronger the wind, the stronger the trees.*
- Willard Marriott -

Priorities

*Do nothing out of selfish
ambition or vain conceit.*
- Philippians 2:3 -

How many times have you heard that someone you know was sick or going through a difficult time and you thought, "Oh, I'm going to give that person a call or send a card"? But, you get busy or time just gets away from you and you never do it. That's a shame, isn't it?

We each are given a number of opportunities to "be God" to someone else ... to show His love and compassion, to be an encourager, and sometimes we just don't do it. Good intentions don't go far in helping another person. As the quote says, if the Good Samaritan only had good intentions but no actions – the man he helped would have died.

We must get beyond the intention stage and put those intentions into action – even when it is inconvenient or when other things are crying for attention. Think about others and how you can be an encouragement and help to them.

*No one would remember the Good Samaritan if he
had only had good intentions, he had money as well.*
- Margaret Thatcher -

New Day ... with History

Because of the Lord's great love we are not consumed, for His compassions never fail. They are new every morning; great is Your faithfulness.

- Lamentations 3:22-23 -

The quote for the day has one part I agree with and one that I don't. It's true that every day with God is new. Every day, every hour, sometimes even every minute is a new submission to Him and a fresh dependence on Him. Every day God brings new experiences and new blessings and new ways to know Him.

But, the part I do not agree with is the second part, "as if nothing has yet been done" because every day that we spend with God we are growing a history of our relationship with Him. So when a new experience presents itself we can look back and see how God strengthened, guided and helped us in a previous situation.

So, while every day is a new start; it is a new start with a history that is growing and developing with each day.

Relying on God has to start all over every day, as if nothing has yet been done.

- C. S. Lewis -

Helping
One Another

Let us consider how we may spur one another on toward love and good deeds.
- Hebrews 10:24 -

Mankind was not meant to live this life alone. We were created by God, who is Himself community – three in one.

He gave instructions in Scripture for us to love one another and help one another. Think about it – when you have really, really good news, what do you want to do? Tell someone who will celebrate with you, right? When you have heartbreaking news, what do you want to do? Tell someone who will cry with you, hug you and pray for you.

Having other people in your life to share the joys and the sorrows of life is so important.

Shared joy is a double joy;
shared sorrow is half a sorrow.
- Swedish Proverb -

Rearview Mirrors

You ought to say, "If it is the Lord's will,
we will live and do this or that."
- James 4:15 -

Looking in the rearview mirror always gives a different perspective on what you've been through. Looking back, you can see how God has worked in your life, guiding, teaching and loving you through various circumstances and stages of life.

So, looking back you may be able to understand why you have had to go through certain trials and that may even make the trials easier to accept. But, life must be lived forward, as the quote says, so going forward, are there things you learned from the past that will help you trust God more in the present and the future? If nothing is learned from the experiences of life then how do you move forward?

Look back, see how God guided you and loved you and then draw on those experiences for the future. That will grow your trust in Him and move you forward in your relationship with Him.

Life can only be understood backwards,
but it must be lived forwards.
- Søren Kierkegaard -

Trials

I don't like to take medicine. Who does, really? The only thing that makes it palatable is that correctly prescribed medicine helps whatever illness my body is fighting to be healed. I have to trust the wisdom of the doctor in diagnosing and prescribing and then it's up to me to take the medicine.

When this illustration is likened to the trials that we go through in life, it makes sense. If the trials are allowed so that I will learn something – to carry out the example – that would mean that some "illness" in my soul (a sinful habit) is cured, then yes, the problems are worth it.

So, as with my physician, I must trust God to know what I need and give exactly the right prescription. Then, I must take my "medicine" and get better ... and thank Him for His medicine.

Trials are medicines which our gracious and wise Physician prescribes because we need them ... Let us trust His skill and thank Him for His prescription.
- Isaac Newton -

Tough Love

Hatred stirs up conflict,
but love covers over all wrongs.
- Proverbs 10:12 -

There is this woman who is driving me crazy! Seriously crazy! If I wanted to get really snarky about it, I would say that she is a brat. But, my grandson says I can't say that word. So, I'll just say that she is self-centered, selfish and just not very nice. Yes, that's better. The bottom line is that she is not a very lovable person. Sigh.

However, the reality is that she really needs my love and acceptance. She is going through some painful stuff, which is what has made her so hard to get along with. It's a good reminder to give difficult people the benefit of the doubt.

Really loving others, as God instructs, means loving them at a time when they are difficult but really need to be loved. My love may be what pulls them out of a depression or what helps get them back on the right track.

What a cool thing to be able to do – however, I'm no saint. I need God to love them through me. He's better at loving the unlovable than I am anyway.

People need loving the most
when they deserve it the least.
- John Harrison -

Moments of Blessings

Give thanks to the Lord, for He is good;
His love endures forever.
- 1 Chronicles 16:34 -

Think about the quote below. Now, think about the title of this book you are reading ... *GodMoments*. Days, weeks, months and years are made up of individual moments. Thousands and thousands of moments.

The good moments – the ones whose memory warms your heart are the God Moments, whether they are moments spent with dear friends, enjoyed with loving family or precious moments with just you and God. He orchestrated each of them. Are you thankful? Do you think to stop in your busy day and just thank Him for the precious moments that you remember?

Thank God for the good memories that bless your heart and give you strength and courage and purpose in moving forward. Thank Him for the moments.

We do not remember days,
we remember moments.
- Cesare Pavese -

Start Small

*"For I was hungry and you gave Me something
to eat, I was thirsty and you gave Me something
to drink, I was a stranger and you invited Me in,
I needed clothes and you clothed Me,
I was sick and you looked after Me,
I was in prison and you came to visit Me."*
- Matthew 25:35-36 -

Some people are blessed to be able to do
amazing things for others because they have a lot
of money or because they are famous and therefore
very prominent.

Have you ever thought about what you would
do if you had a lot of money, time or power to
help others in the world? Perhaps you've thought
that you would be amazingly generous and compassionate.

Not many of us get those big opportunities.
But, we do have small opportunities every day to
be kind, helpful and generous to those in our own
neighborhoods and communities. Start there – be
examples of God's generosity and love.

Take a risk and put yourself in situations that
are out of your comfort zone. See how God can use
you to bless others. If you are faithful in the small
opportunities, God may open bigger ones!

*Great opportunities to help others seldom come,
but small ones surround us every day.*
- Sally Koch -

Encouragement of Friends

A friend loves at all times,
and a brother is born for a time of adversity.
- Proverbs 17:17 -

We all need a little help once in a while – not just physical help, but emotional support also. That's why God gives us friends – Christian brothers and sisters who can help us find our way when we are feeling lost.

When you come to a place where life is weighing you down and it even feels a little hopeless, true friends can help you find your way again. True friends know you, your values, your dreams, the way you've been going, and that friend will keep lifting you up, encouraging, challenging, helping you get back on track.

In many ways, these types of friends are like "God with skin on" because He uses them to be His voice and His touch. Thank God for these kinds of friends.

A friend knows the song in my heart and
sings it to me when my memory fails.
- Donna Roberts -

A Second of Thankfulness

*Enter His gates with thanksgiving
and His courts with praise;
give thanks to Him and praise His name.*
- Psalm 100:4 -

One young grandson is very good at saying, "Thank you." Whatever is done for him from filling his juice cup to helping put on his shoes to finding his missing toy, his response is always, "Thank you." The other grandson often has to be reminded to say thanks. He willingly says these magic words when reminded. He just doesn't think of it as readily as his brother does. How many of us are more like the second grandson?

We do not readily thank God for the blessings He pours out on us. Of course, if reminded, we gladly thank Him. But, why doesn't thankfulness enter our minds immediately? Have we come to expect God's blessings? Are we so self-absorbed that we ignore His generosity?

We are daily given seconds, minutes and hours, let's use some of them to thank God that He gives so much to us each and every day.

*God gave you a gift of 86,400 seconds today.
Have you used one to say "thank you?"*
- William A. Ward -

Kind God Moments

Be kind and compassionate to one another,
forgiving each other, just as in
Christ God forgave you.
- Ephesians 4:32 -

Sitting in a hospital room watching over a sick loved one is exhausting; physically, emotionally and mentally. Day after day. Night after night. The uncertainty and the loneliness begin to play with your mind.

What an act of kindness for someone to step forward and say, "I live nearby. Come spend the night at my house." I'm no longer alone with my fears. I've got someone to talk with!

Opportunities for kindness come in many ways – big and small. It takes putting yourself in someone else's situation and thinking about what they might need. Then, taking those thoughts and allowing God to show you how to put them into action.

An act of kindness often becomes a God Moment for the one receiving the kindness. What a privilege to be on the other end!

I expect to pass through life but once. If therefore,
there be any kindness I can show, or any good thing
I can do to any fellow being, let me do it now.
- William Penn -

Consumed by Envy

A heart at peace gives life to the body,
but envy rots the bones.
- Proverbs 14:30

Consumed is an interesting word. When I'm consumed by something, I can't think about much else. Every thought, every action is affected by that thing that is consuming me. When that thing is a bad thing – such as envy of another person – it pretty much ruins my life. It eats away at me until my conversation is completely focused on that envy.

My usefulness to others is compromised. My friendships are damaged. My own self-esteem is wrecked. It's not pretty. Where does envy come from? The root of it is self-centeredness in the sense that God owes me whatever anyone else has that I want.

It's a dissatisfaction with God and the way He made me and what He gave me. That's pretty serious and is something that must be dealt with in order to have a healthier life and relationship with Him.

As iron is eaten by rust,
so are the envious consumed by envy.
- Antisthenes -

Prayers in the Good Times

Do not be anxious about anything, but in every situation, by prayer and petition, with thanksgiving, present your requests to God.
- Philippians 4:6 -

When life goes sour we are quick to hop on the prayer train, aren't we? We pray and pray and nag and beg and instruct and cry for God's attention to us and to our problem. There's nothing wrong with that, in fact, God tells us to pray. He wants to hear the cries of our hearts.

But what happens when life is going well? When we have no crises and things are going pretty much as we would hope? Do we still pray with the same fervency? Do we thank? Do we praise? Do we acknowledge His goodness to us? Do we appreciate His care? We should, you know.

Our conversations with God should be in the good times as well as in the hard times. He doesn't want to just be our problem solver. He wants to be a part of our lives.

Don't pray when it rains if you don't pray when the sun shines.
- Satchel Paige -

What Are You Waiting For?

Not that I have already obtained all this,
or have already arrived at my goal,
but I press on to take hold of that
for which Christ Jesus took hold of me.
- Philippians 3:12 -

Do you have a case of the "somedays?" What is that, you ask? It's the explanation you hear from people who are not yet "in the game" of doing what God wants them to do. The "someday" condition goes something like this ... "Yeah, I know God has called me to full-time ministry and I'm going to do that as soon as my school bills are paid off." Or, "God is leading me to the mission field and I will go as soon as I get married."

The "somedays" can take so many identities, but the bottom line for those with this condition is that they spend so much time working toward getting ready to serve or obey that the work they are supposed to be doing never gets done. That's pretty sad, isn't it?

God gave you something to do – don't make excuses and don't spend all your time getting ready to do it. Just get busy.

I have spent my days stringing
and unstringing my instrument,
while the song I came to sing remains unsung.
- Rabindranath Tagore -

Basic Thankfulness

*Always giving thanks to
God the Father for everything,
in the name of our Lord Jesus Christ.*
- Ephesians 5:20 -

Children love Christmas. At least the children who know they will get gifts love Christmas. The anticipation is so much fun and the process of opening gifts almost puts kids over the edge. Of course there is the whole "writing thank you notes" to bring them back to reality. But, it's good to remind kids to be thankful to those who take the time to choose gifts for them and try to find gifts they will really like.

It is a good habit to learn to say thank you and not take any kindnesses for granted. God has given each of us so much and it seems that the more we have, the more we expect and our gratefulness slips lower and lower.

Take time to thank God today. Thank Him for the basic things of life – the things you don't usually even think about.

*When we were children we were grateful
to those who filled our stockings at Christmas time.
Why are we not grateful to God for
filling our stockings with legs?*
- G. K. Chesterton -

Stuck

Those who live according to the flesh have
their minds set on what the flesh desires;
but those who live in accordance
with the Spirit have their minds
set on what the Spirit desires.
- Romans 8:5 -

Some people are stubbornly narrow-minded. They have made judgments and hold beliefs that were developed years and years ago and they will not, under any circumstances, let those beliefs waver. Is that wise?

As we grow and mature and as things change around us, some beliefs will probably also change (not the foundational things, of course).

However, some people get so comfortable with where they are that they will not even consider adjusting their beliefs. They become boxed in. It's kind of sad, really. Because, this stubbornness limits God from teaching and growing compassionate and considerate hearts in these people. They are stuck in a time warp and can't see what new things God may want to teach them. So sad.

An old belief is like an old shoe. We so value its
comfort that we fail to notice the hole in it.
- Robert Brault -

How to Respond

*Do not say, "I'll do to them as they have done
to me; I'll pay them back for what they did."*
- Proverbs 24:29 -

If you're going to work with people, you're going to get hurt once in a while. You will sometimes be the victim of rude and unkind comments and of unfair judgments. That's just the way it is once in a while. And pretty much all of us work or live with people, so it will come!

Ruth Graham's advice is very practical and very Christlike. Pray for a tough hide so that those unkind comments will roll off, then you won't react and say or do things to hurt the other person. Pray for a tender heart so that God can show you what brought on the actions or words from the other person.

He or she may be dealing with some pretty intense things which spurred the action toward you. Pray that you can respond in love and thus "be the love of God" in your response.

Just pray for a tough hide and a tender heart.
- Ruth Graham -

Originality

*I praise You because I am fearfully
and wonderfully made; Your works
are wonderful, I know that full well.*
- Psalm 139:14 -

Like-minded people tend to hang out together. We tend to join churches where we agree with each other's beliefs. We choose our friends in the same way. It certainly makes for a more peaceful life, doesn't it? But, if you aren't sometimes challenged, there is a danger that you may grow stale and habitual in life.

People who all believe the same things, live in the same pattern and do the same things, become able to anticipate one another. They begin to do things out of habit rather than conviction.

God made you an individual with unique ideas, talents, dreams and beliefs. Of course you will agree with some people on some things, but don't allow yourself to get into a rut that makes you a copy of those around you and takes away your individuality. Be you. That's who God made.

*You were born an original.
Don't die a copy.*
- John Mason -

Be Still

He says, "Be still, and know that I am God;
I will be exalted among the nations,
I will be exalted in the earth."
- Psalm 46:10 -

Silence is not easy to find in our busy lives. We run from the busyness of family to church, work, friends, housework, yardwork and back to family. If you think to turn the radio off in the car, that may be the only time of silence in your day.

Even when you settle down to pray, most of the time you don't make time for silence. Prayer time is spent in making intercession for others (a good thing), asking for God's help (also a good thing), and seeking His guidance (a very good thing). Then we pop out a quick "Amen" before we're off and running again. When is He supposed to answer?

Maybe silence makes us uncomfortable, but sitting in silence before God is the perfect time to hear His voice and sense His guidance. That's why He tells us to "be still."

God speaks in the silence of the heart.
Listening is the beginning of prayer.
- Mother Teresa -

Those Who Have Gone Before ...

*You know how we lived among you
for your sake. You became imitators
of us and of the Lord, for you welcomed
the message in the midst of severe suffering
with the joy given by the Holy Spirit.*
- 1 Thessalonians 1:5-7 -

Our society seems more and more to devalue older people. Some cultures treasure their elderly. They care for them with respect and honor. They listen to them and learn from them. There is great wisdom in that, particularly from a spiritual point of view.

Mature Christians have lived through life situations and learned from them. They have experienced God and have seen how He works and how He relates to His people. Just as we read Scripture to see how God led, taught and blessed His people, we can learn the same things from older believers who have a history with Him.

Cultivate friendships with older believers in your church. See what you can learn from them. Pray with them and ask them to pray for you. You will learn much.

To know the road ahead, ask those coming back.
- Chinese Proverb -

No "Little People"

"So in everything, do to others what you would have them do to you, for this sums up the Law and the Prophets."
- Matthew 7:12 -

Sometimes people get way too full of themselves. I suppose it comes partly from being prideful added to super busy and the feeling that they don't have the time to give to "little people."

You know who the little people are ... anyone who has nothing to offer to these super important, super busy people. They are pretty much ignored because they appear to be pretty much useless. Remember the folk tale of the lion and the mouse? It was the mouse who saved the lion from a trap because the lion had done a kind deed for the mouse.

It could pay to be kind to those you may secretly consider "little people." They could actually be the ones who can be a friend to you in the future. In fact, it pays to be kind to everyone ... it is the way of Jesus.

Be nice to those you meet on the way up.
They're the same folks you'll meet on the way down.
- Walter Winchell -

Don't Trust Feelings

*All Scripture is God-breathed and
is useful for teaching, rebuking,
correcting and training in righteousness.*
- 2 Timothy 3:16-17 -

Too often our faith rests on feelings.
Granted, it's difficult to keep feelings from affecting our faith because we are feeling people. God made us that way.

Things that happen in our lives bring good feelings or bad feelings and often our outlook and attitude are based on those feelings. But it's not a good thing to allow feelings to dictate faith things, because faith is based on fact – not feeling.

The promises of Scripture tell us of God's care, power, and protection for His children. In fact, Scripture promises those things to us. Feelings will try to convince us that none of that is true. We need to be careful which feelings we allow to run rampant in our hearts. We shouldn't trust the feelings that deny the things we know are true.

We must trust God. We must trust Scripture ... feelings come and go. Scripture stands forever.

Feelings are much like waves, we can't stop them from coming but we can choose which one to surf.
- Jonatan Mårtensson -

True Thankfulness

Give thanks in all circumstances;
for this is God's will for you in Christ Jesus.
- 1 Thessalonians 5:18 -

Wow. Read and think about today's quote below. The Pilgrims were a group of people who left their homeland, families, way of life and safety and sailed to a new continent to begin a new life and one major reason was that they wanted religious freedom.

They arrived in their new land and faced all kinds of hardships and dangers – many, many of the Pilgrims died before getting established here. And yet, they set aside a day in their year to just be thankful. How about that? Does this speak to you?

It's so easy to focus on the negatives in our lives and never take time to thank God for the positives. No matter how difficult or stressful life gets, God is with you. Loving, protecting, guiding, blessing – you have no idea how much if you're only focusing on the bad things. Set aside a personal day for just thanking Him. It will change your whole attitude!

The Pilgrims made seven times more
graves than huts. No Americans have
been more impoverished than these who,
nevertheless, set aside a day of thanksgiving.
- H. U. Westermayer -

The Value of Friends

No one has ever seen God; but if we love one another, God lives in us and His love is made complete in us.
- 1 John 4:12 -

Friends. What would life be without friends? If you have good friends who pick you up when you are down, cry with you, laugh with you, celebrate with you or just be with you, then you are truly blessed.

Friends can definitely bring God's presence to you in a human, physical, hugging, crying, laughing way. The struggles of life are much more oppressive if you have no one with whom to share them. But to have friends, you must also be a friend.

So, all the things you value in your friends are things that you can be to them, also. It's a two-way street. So, thank God for your friends. Thank your friends for their friendship. And, be as good a friend to them as they are to you.

If you want a hug, I'll be your pillow.
If you need to be happy, I'll be your smile.
But anytime you need a friend, I'll just be me.
- Anonymous -

Honest Friendships

"A new command I give you:
Love one another. As I have loved you,
so you must love one another."
- John 13:34 -

If you've ever walked around the outside of your home and noticed little piles of sawdust, you know the sinking feeling of TERMITES! The little critters come and chow down on the wood of YOUR house. Their chomping makes holes in the wood so it isn't as sturdy or safe for you and your family.

If we liken assumptions to termites, then they make holes in relationships that destroy the depth and trust of friendships. What are assumptions? They are things you decide are true, but you don't have any facts to back up those decisions. Assumptions usually decide the worst about friends and their intentions. So, without discussing assumptions made, holes are poked in friendships and serious damage is done.

The lesson here is when you assume there are problems, talk with your friends and get the truth. Remember that God instructs you to love those around you. Make that your focus.

Assumptions are the termites of relationships.
- Henry Winkler -

God Wants to Hear from You

This is the confidence we have in
approaching God: that if we ask
anything according to His will, He hears us.
And if we know that He hears us –
whatever we ask – we know that
we have what we asked of Him.
- 1 John 5:14, 15 -

God didn't have to do it – He didn't have to open Himself up to conversation with His creation. But He did. He not only offers us the privilege of prayer, He commands us to talk with Him. It seems that God wants to know how we feel about whatever is going on in our lives. Unfortunately, too often our prayer life is most active when we have major problems. We just want God to fix things for us or make us feel better.

From what we read in Scripture, we know that God had something more in mind for our prayer lives. If we pray only when we have problems, we miss the depth of a relationship that God hoped our prayer life would build with Him.

Think about it – God didn't have to offer you the privilege of prayer but He did ... because He wants to have a relationship with you.

Many people pray as if God were a big aspirin pill;
they come only when they hurt.
- B. Graham Dienert -

Proof

Some would have you believe that sin isn't so bad. They would try to convince you that a loving God would not truly condemn you just because of sin. But, the evidence says something else.

Jesus, God's own Son, came to earth as part of a plan to die for the sins of humankind so that we could, one day, be clean enough to be in His presence. So ... sin must matter.

The coolest thing though is that Jesus didn't stay dead, He came back to life. God's complete loving forgiveness is evident through the living Jesus.

Take sin seriously, ask His forgiveness and trust God's love to be evident in your life. Thank Him for His grace and forgiveness.

The dying Jesus is the evidence of God's
anger toward sin; but the living Jesus
is the proof of God's love and forgiveness.
- Lorenz Eifert -

Open Your Mouth

Give praise to the Lord, proclaim His name;
make known among the nations what He has done.
- 1 Chronicles 16:8 -

You go out of your way to do something nice for someone. And, yeah, it was a sacrifice of your time and effort and maybe even your finances. You were glad to do it though.

But, let's be honest ... it would have been nice to be thanked. You may know that the recipient of your kindness is truly thankful, but just didn't make the effort or take the time to tell you.

Silent gratitude is OK ... but it doesn't encourage a relationship because the person who extends the kindness doesn't hear the gratitude. Of course, when you do something kind, you don't do it for the thanks, but it's nice to hear it once in a while.

Imagine how God feels. He does so much for you ... every single day. Take time to SAY thank You to Him. Do not let your gratitude be silent!

Silent gratitude isn't much use to anyone.
- G. B. Stern -

Water Walker?

*Know therefore that the Lord your
God is God; He is the faithful God,
keeping His covenant of love to a
thousand generations of those who
love Him and keep His commandments.*

- Deuteronomy 7:9 -

Jesus is awesome! Read through the New
Testament to learn about His amazing miracles.
Those miracles leave you stunned by their power.
One of the most incredible miracles was when
Jesus walked on the water to get to the boat His
disciples were sailing in. It showed His power over
nature and His love and concern for His friends.

It's a very cool story of who Jesus is. And, He's
your Savior so His power and strength are available
to you. But as today's quote says, what good is it
to have such an awesome, powerful Savior if you
don't follow Him?

Following Him means learning from Him and
obeying His teachings. Don't be a name-only Jesus
follower. Be a learning, obeying, close follower.
Who knows, maybe He will help you walk on
water!

*What good is having someone who can walk
on water if you don't follow in His footsteps?*

- Anonymous -

Grabbing an Opportunity

Consider it pure joy, my brothers and sisters, whenever you face trials of many kinds, because you know that the testing of your faith produces perseverance. Let perseverance finish its work so that you may be mature and complete, not lacking anything.

- James 1:2-4 -

Most of us do not face the danger and stress of a crisis looking for some incredible opportunity. The usual response to a crisis is to get out of it as quickly as we can. The thought of finding opportunity in the crisis is far from our minds.

But it makes sense that by turning to God we can grow in strength and faith and by that, realize positive opportunities from the crisis. Maybe you think, "I can't do that. It's too hard." Never fear, God will help you find the strength and courage to face a crisis and see the opportunity in it.

He will help you grow stronger in your walk with Christ, deeper in your faith and more trusting in the power of prayer. Crisis usually means change and that change can mean growth and development.

When written in Chinese the word crisis is composed of two characters – one represents danger and the other represents opportunity.

- John F. Kennedy -

Safety Net Friends

Therefore encourage one another and build
each other up, just as in fact you are doing.
- 1 Thessalonians 5:11 -

Circus high-wire performers are thrilling to watch. The risks they take and the athletic skills they perform while perched on a thin little wire high above the crowd is amazing. Once in a very great while (not often) one of the performers will miss a step and fall. The crowd gasps in horror ... until the performer lands in the safety net strung below the high wire.

Our friends are like safety nets. Their support, help and encouragement catch us when we fall. Their challenges and accountability keep us walking close to God. Friends we can depend on in the hard times are truly a gift from God.

Pray for your friends, thank God for them. Thank them for their friendship and encouragement. And do your best to be that kind of friend to others.

It is not so much our friends' help that helps us,
as the confidence of their help.
- Epicurus -

Getting Busy

*Command those who are rich in this present
world not to be arrogant nor to put their
hope in wealth, which is so uncertain, but to
put their hope in God, who richly provides
us with everything for our enjoyment.*
- 1 Timothy 6:17 -

I know a woman who worries about absolutely everything. She worries about things that have already happened, things that might happen and things that would never happen in a thousand years. She literally makes herself ill by worry. But the thing is, she doesn't do anything to help the situations she is worried about.

Granted, some things are beyond human help and rest fully in God's hands. But sometimes there are things that we can do to help situations. Perhaps the reason that particular situation weighs so heavily on our hearts is that God placed it there so we would get up and help.

So, if something is really bothering you, stop wringing your hands, take a cue that this may be from God, roll up your sleeves and get busy helping!

*You can't wring your hands and roll
up your sleeves at the same time.*
- Pat Schroeder -

Problem Fighter

"If you have faith as small as a mustard seed, you can say to this mulberry tree, 'Be uprooted and planted in the sea,' and it will obey you."

- Luke 17:6 -

Wouldn't it be great if, once you accepted Jesus as your Savior, life was just one easy cruise to heaven? Yes, that would make life so comfortable! Everyone would want to become a Christian with such a promise of no more problems.

Whoa – back to reality. Having faith in Jesus does not take away our problems. He never promised that it would. He just promised that we would never be alone with our problems. He would always be with us, helping us and strengthening us.

So ... yes, you have problems. But your faith in Jesus means that it is possible to overcome the problems ... with His help!

Faith makes things possible, not easy.
- Anonymous -

Unprecedented Worship

*Worship the Lord with gladness;
come before Him with joyful songs.*
- Psalm 100:2 -

Acquiescence means that a person gives agreement with no argument. That's pretty cool, isn't it? Our worship comes because our mind completely agrees to the reality of God, with no argument. Once we come into God's presence and realize His greatness and power and His total, unconditional love for us, there is nothing else to do but worship Him.

Worship begins with admitting God's greatness and continues with our adoration of who He is. It's praise, adoration, love, submission and joy at the fact of who God is. Worship flows from us with no questions, regrets or complaints.

We worship because of who God is. Have you done that lately? Have you just worshiped without questions, complaints or anything else – just worshiped the greatness and love of God?

*Worship is the mind's humble
acquiescence to the fact of God.*
- Peter C. Moore -

The Power of Love

We love because He first loved us.
- 1 John 4:19 -

The evening news is about the most depressing program on TV. Story after story of murders, robberies, rapes, wars, terrorist attacks ... man's inhumanity to man. Too many of these stories stem from one person or group wanting power over another person or group. The evening news does not often carry stories that show the power of love. That's the work of God and His people.

We must live our lives filled with the power of love so that it flows to all those around us. That love is contagious. Once others see it flowing freely, they will copy it and the power of love will spread.

Peace will follow that love and the ability to get along with others – even those we disagree with. It's possible. Let the love begin with you!

We look forward to the time when the power of love will replace the love of power. Then will our world know the blessings of peace.
- William Ewart Gladstone -

It's Complicated

*The Lord God said, "It is not good
for the man to be alone. I will
make a helper suitable for him."*
- Genesis 2:18 -

The relationships of family and even friendship can get complicated. There are certainly the joys of the support and love that are shared in these relationships. However, there are also the complications that arise when the decisions made by one person impact another.

What this points out is that we are intertwined with the other people in our world. That's a good thing – God Himself said that it is not good for man to be alone. He made us to live in community, with family or with a group of friends.

Together we can stand strong. Together we can encourage one another. Together we challenge each other to stand strong for God and to grow deeper in Him. We need each other. So, celebrate your group and don't try to go it alone. It's easier with others!

*No man is an island, entire of itself;
every man is a piece of the continent.*
- John Donne -

Bundle Up!

*Two are better than one, because they have
a good return for their labor: If either of
them falls down, one can help the other up.
But pity anyone who falls and
has no one to help them up.*
- Ecclesiastes 4:9-10 -

A single stick that falls from a tree into your yard can be picked up and snapped in two with no problem. Two sticks together are a little harder to break, but it's still possible. But, if you pick up a whole bundle of sticks, they cannot be broken all at the same time. A bundle of sticks together is stronger than one single stick.

Guess what God knew? One person by herself can be tempted, broken or pulled away from faith. It is much more difficult to stand strong when you are alone. But, several friends together can help one another be strong. They battle weaknesses together and encourage one another to stay close to God.

Seek out your like-minded family and friends and "bundle up." Stay close and stay strong.

Sticks in a bundle are unbreakable.
- Kenyan Proverb -

What Is Your Mark?

Above all, love each other deeply,
because love covers over a multitude of sins.
- 1 Peter 4:8 -

The Scriptures say that the love God's children show to others is what should make them stand out in this world. It should make us different from the rest of the world. How are we doing with that?

Love should always be our theme; even when we disagree with another person or are attacked by someone. Our response, even in disagreement or correction should always be couched with love. Unfortunately, some Christians portray a judgmental attitude, criticism and separateness that shows no love at all. We can take our stand and stay separate from the world, but do so with a loving attitude.

Love is shown by attitude, tone of voice, and choice of words. Let love be your motivation. That's what shows the world who you belong to!

We have learned to fly the air like birds and swim
the sea like fish, but we have not learned
the simple art of living together as brothers.
- Martin Luther King, Jr -

God's Constant Presence

Have I not commanded you? Be strong and
courageous. Do not be afraid; do not be
discouraged, for the Lord your God
will be with you wherever you go.
- Joshua 1:9 -

Let's be honest ... sometimes it "feels" as though God is absent. It "feels" as though He is not paying attention and perhaps doesn't know what you are going through. Of course, in your heart you know that isn't true. But, you can "feel" alone for so long that you begin to wonder.

Trust Scripture. It tells us that God is with us, always and forever, wherever we may go. There is an old saying that the will of God will not lead you where the grace of God cannot keep you. In other words, God is everywhere, and therefore is always with you. He knows what you're facing and He has not turned His back.

So, keep trusting. Keep holding on to His promises, even when you can't "feel" His presence. He is there.

God's center is everywhere,
His circumference is nowhere.
- Henry Law -

Work of Love

Vacation Bible School was a big deal at our church. Hundreds of children came and dozens of workers gave a lot of hours to it. One particular woman comes to mind when I think about those VBS days. She was there every day, year after year. She seldom smiled. She seldom had a nice word to say.

The children were afraid of her and the other workers gave her a wide berth. It never felt as though she "wanted" to be there. Not much love flowed from her. So, what does that mean? She was dedicated. She was dependable. But the lack of love flowing from her inhibited her ministry.

Love ... it's so important in your actions and in your words. It is even more important than what you do.

God regards with how much love a person performs a work, rather than how much he does.
- Thomas à Kempis -

Personal Praise

The heavens declare the glory of God;
the skies proclaim the work of His hands.
- Psalm 19:1 -

God speaks to different people in different ways. Some people feel closest to Him while reading His Word. The stories of how He worked in people's lives, guiding, protecting and loving them comfort their hearts. The promises of His love and protection are very precious.

Some people feel close to God in the great cathedral of nature. The majestic mountains and the grand oceans speak to them of God's creative power. The gentle forests, shaded with trees, carpeted by pine needles, dotted with colorful flowers speak of God's loving care. All of creation sings of God's glory.

Where is the place that most speaks to your heart? Do you go there often to have your own personal worship service? Praise to God is a beautiful, precious, individual song.

God writes the gospel not in the Bible alone,
but on trees, and flowers, and clouds and stars.
- Martin Luther -

A Good Life

"For whoever wants to save their life will lose it, but whoever loses their life for Me will find it."
- Matthew 16:25 -

What is your legacy? No one gets out of this life alive (unless Jesus comes back) so, once you leave this life, what will people remember about you?

It will not be things like how many hours you worked, or how much money you made. Those are success markers that the world puts on people, but they don't last. What would you like your legacy to be?

The Bible tells us over and over that what is truly important is knowing and serving God – giving your life over to Him to be marked by serving and loving others with a humble heart. You can live to be 110 but if you haven't given your life to God to be used by Him in whatever way He chooses, then you have missed the mark. Serve Him. Love Him. Serve others. Love others.

The measure of a life, after all, is not its duration, but its donation.
- Corrie ten Boom -

God's Priority

*Children are a heritage from the Lord,
offspring a reward from Him.*
- Psalm 127:3 -

Everyone has a family – some by birth and some by choice. The family you grew up in helped to mold and shape you into the person you have become. The family you have established as an adult is continuing that work and molding and shaping your children, too.

If you don't have a family, the one you have created, made up of friends, also forms you and is your secure, safe place.

Families are important. God made them because He knew that a healthy family is a safe place where we are taught how to live amongst other people. That doesn't mean we don't have differences. We do. It doesn't mean we won't hurt each other. We will. It means that we love one another, forgive one another and stand by one another whatever comes. What a gift from God!

*The family was ordained by God before
He established any other institution,
even before He established the church.*
- Billy Graham -

Evil Hearts

*God is faithful; He will not let you
be tempted beyond what you can bear.
But when you are tempted, He will also
provide a way out so that you can endure it.*
- 1 Corinthians 10:13 -

You never really know what is lurking in your heart until you are tempted. You may be convinced of your goodness and morals but you don't really know what you are capable of until the opportunity comes to cheat or hurt or sin in some way you never imagined, particularly if it seems that no one would know about it.

The Bible tells us that we are all sinners. We all have wicked hearts. It is by the goodness and grace of God that we are forgiven and can have the hope of heaven.

But, in the meantime, on this earth, we need to ask God to cleanse our hearts and deliver us from every temptation that Satan will drive our way. He wants us to fail at living for God. But, God wants us to succeed. So go to Him humbly and often, and ask for His help in resisting temptation. He will clean up your heart because He wants you to succeed.

*Temptation is the fire that brings
up the scum of the heart.*
- William Shakespeare -

Choose Discipline

Those who hope in the Lord
will renew their strength.
They will soar on wings like eagles;
they will run and not grow weary,
they will walk and not be faint.

- Isaiah 40:31 -

"It's too hard," my three-year-old grandson moans when I ask him to pick up his toys. The discipline I inflict by asking him to clean up seems to him to weigh tons. I wonder how often I behave with that same sort of resistance when it comes to adult-sized discipline?

The discipline to do what's right, such as apologize to someone I've wronged, or serve in some way I've been called, or make the effort to visit distant relatives. What about the discipline of daily time with God?

Discipline speaks of work but it is work that will make me a better person and a better servant of God. Not obeying the need for discipline will someday lead to regret which lays on the heart like a thousand pound weight. There isn't much you can do to get rid of it except remember to choose discipline the next time the opportunity arises.

Discipline weighs ounces, regret weighs tons.
- Anonymous -

Healthy Lives

Your word is a lamp for my feet,
a light on my path.
- Psalm 119:105 -

My teenage son had a voracious appetite. Seriously, the boy was a bottomless pit. We had to take out a loan just to keep him in food. However, his appetite had a restlessness. While he may have chosen junk food such as chips, cookies, pizza and soda, those things didn't satisfy his appetite because they didn't provide the nutrition his body needed to grow.

Does your spirit have an appetite like that? Do you hunger to know God better? Do you yearn to grow closer to Him? Do you long to be more and more like Christ? That's the appetite God has planted in you – to make you more and more into the person He sees and has planned for you to be.

Eat healthily then – from His Word and from your prayer life with Him. That's the healthy food that will grow you to maturity.

God plants in us an appetite for growth.
That appetite creates a restlessness
dissatisfied with anything less than maturity.
- Jeannette Clift George -

Convenient Temptations

It [Grace of God] teaches us to say "No"
to ungodliness and worldly passions,
and to live self-controlled, upright
and godly lives in this present age.
- Titus 2:12 -

How serious are you about obeying God? You can fool people by making grand announcements and taking prominent stands against certain sins. But what happens in the privacy of your own heart? If there is a certain temptation you struggle with ... say it's Internet porn ... how far away do you put it? Do you ask God to deliver you from this sin but keep a record of the websites?

If your temptation is gossip or alcohol or whatever it is ... do you stay away from the opportunity to indulge in it, or do you secretly keep it close so that it is available should you want it?

God wants your complete obedience – realizing that there will be times when you fail, because after all, you are human. But, deliberately keeping the opportunity for secret sins close at hand ... well, that is not obedience.

Most people want to be delivered from
temptation but would like it to keep in touch.
- Robert Orben -

"I" Trouble

*"Do to others as you would
have them do to you."*
- Luke 6:31 -

The problem with much of the world today is "I" trouble. There is a self-centeredness among many people who think "I" need to have it all.

So, with no concern for those who do not have anything to eat, "I" want more than my share. With no concern for those who have no place to live, "I" want a bigger and better home. With no concern for those who do not have the basic necessities of life, "I" want a bigger TV and a fancier car and the newest cellphone. "I" just doesn't pay much attention to the rest of the world.

Is this what God intended for all of us humans who inhabit this planet? No, He wanted us to take care of one another, share with one another and love one another. How are we doing?

*I have often noticed that when chickens quit
quarreling over their food they often find
that there is enough for all of them.*
- Don Marquis -

Live Now

*Being confident of this, that He who began
a good work in you will carry it on to
completion until the day of Christ Jesus.*
- Philippians 1:6 -

What have you done for God lately?
What has God done for you lately? If you answer
either of these questions with a story from five years
ago, something is missing from your life. The past
is a wonderful thing but it is over and done with.

Is your relationship with God alive and vibrant
enough that you see Him in each day? Is your
devotion to Him real enough that you serve Him
each day? Remember the past and learn from it,
but live in today and use it.

Look around you today and see evidence of
God's presence in your life. It's there. Look around
and see opportunities to serve Him today. They
are there. Keep your relationship with God alive
enough that your stories of Him in your life are
current and shows that you are growing in Him
every day!

*If you are still talking about what you did
yesterday, you haven't done much today.*
- Anonymous -

Joy-Filled Hearts

Rejoice always.
- 1 Thessalonians 5:16 -

An attitude of joy is catching. A person who is filled with joy does not get weighed down by the struggles of life. She can honestly admit when things in her life are difficult – no rose-colored glasses here. But, no matter how difficult life gets, she is able to focus on the blessings of life rather than the problems. She always has hope.

So then, people who are around her find encouragement and hope from her joyful outlook. It is hard to keep being negative when joy flows so freely.

Joy like this speaks loudly of a full-hearted trust in God. It says that God is ultimately in control so whatever else happens, you can trust that God has a plan and that that plan is ultimately for your good. What a wonderful way to live!

One filled with joy preaches without preaching.
- Mother Teresa -

No Excuses!

I can do all this through
Him who gives me strength.
- Philippians 4:13 -

Excuses are the roadblocks to progress. The person who truly has a desire to accomplish something will persist through all kinds of struggles. He will find a way to succeed and will not make excuses for his failures. This is the person whom God can use in amazing ways because a little problem doesn't make him quit, and big problems don't faze him either.

What type of person are you? Do you work at something for a while, but when the going gets tough, you get going? Can God count on you to stick with the challenge of the work He gives you rather than making excuses for why you give up? Remember, His strength will help you so turn to Him rather than to excuses.

He that is good for making excuses
is seldom good for anything else.
- Benjamin Franklin -

Live Well!

I sat beside a dear friend as she left this life and entered the gates of heaven. Her departing was peaceful and in some ways I believe she anticipated it. She knew she was going to be with God. She had nothing to fear about that new phase of her existence because she had lived her life well.

Was she famous? No. Was she wealthy? No. At least neither of those were true by the world's standards. She was famous among her friends for her love and compassion and for her devotion to God. She was wealthy in friends and blessings from God.

This is a reminder to live your life fully in God. Give Him each day and live each one in love and service to Him. Then, when this life ends, you will have only anticipation!

*The fear of death follows from the fear of life.
A man who lives fully is prepared to die at any time.*
- Mark Twain -

Reach Out to Others

Do you know the 4:00 AM loneliness when you wake up and can't get back to sleep? Everyone else is sleeping (as far as you know) and as you lie there, wide awake, with only the stress that woke you to keep you company ... you feel lonely. Facing life and feeling that you have no one to share it with and that no one even cares is true loneliness. The flip side of that is having no one to care about.

Caring is a two-way street – it feels good to be cared for and it feels good to care because then you're needed. If you're feeling lonely the best thing to do is reach out to someone.

Ask God to bring someone across your path who also needs a friend. Then, take a risk and reach out to be a friend to someone.

Loneliness is the most terrible poverty.
- Mother Teresa -

Guilty of Neglect

Praise the Lord. I will extol the Lord
with all my heart in the council of
the upright and in the assembly.
Great are the works of the Lord;
they are pondered by all who delight in them.
- Psalm 111:1-2 -

Dear Father, I'm guilty, OK? I admit it. There have been like a million times when I've just accepted the blessings in my life without even a thought of gratitude. In fact, to make it worse, I have come to expect more and more blessings and to feel cheated or even angry if I do not get them.

I'm sorry. I really am. You give me so much every day and just at this moment, I recognize that. So, please forgive me and then accept my incredible gratitude. I'm so thankful for Your love, Your provision, Your protection, Your gifts of family, friends, home ... but most of all I'm thankful for Jesus and the salvation I enjoy because of Him.

Thank You for loving me enough to make a plan. I promise to remember to be thankful ... and say it. Amen.

There is no such thing as gratitude unexpressed. If it
is unexpressed, it is plain, old-fashioned ingratitude.
- Robert Brault -

Persevere!

*Make every effort to add to your faith
goodness; and to goodness, knowledge;
and to knowledge, self-control; and to
self-control, perseverance; and to perseverance,
godliness; and to godliness, mutual affection;
and to mutual affection, love.*
- 2 Peter 1:5-7 -

Scripture often sings the praises of perseverance and the good lessons learned from it. Perseverance in our Christian faith makes that faith stronger and teaches us good lessons of obedience.

But, what is important to remember is that there is a negative version of perseverance and it is called obstinacy or stubbornness. It is a version of perseverance that keeps people from obeying God because they want to make their own calls and live their own lives – independent of God.

Yes, God gives us freedom to make our own choices but He also has given us Scripture that teaches us the way to live in obedience to Him and in a way that will help us live more peacefully with others. Persevere to be obedient to God but do not be obstinate in obeying God.

*The difference between perseverance and
obstinacy is that one comes from a strong will,
and the other from a strong won't.*
- Henry Ward Beecher -

Forgiveness Accepted

Once you were alienated from God and
were enemies in your minds because of your
evil behavior. But now He has reconciled
you by Christ's physical body through
death to present you holy in His sight,
without blemish and free from accusation.
- Colossians 1:21-22 -

I have a friend who is very hard on himself. He does not give himself permission to fail or make mistakes. He expects great things from himself and his standards are very high.

Of course, it's a good thing to have high standards and to work hard but if a person can't forgive himself for failures, it makes it much more difficult to accept God's forgiveness. His forgiveness is filled with grace and with the encouragement to keep on moving forward.

Are you able to forgive yourself when you fail? Can you learn what God wants to teach you from failures? Failure is part of life and provides a great opportunity to learn and grow. So, cut yourself some slack, forgive yourself, learn, thank God for His forgiveness and move on!

No one is perfect ...
that's why pencils have erasers.
- Anonymous -

Use Your Talents

So Christ Himself gave the apostles,
the prophets, the evangelists,
the pastors and teachers,
to equip His people for works of service,
so that the body of Christ may be built up.
- Ephesians 4:11-12 -

God gives every person talents and abilities. Not everyone is the same but every one is necessary to spread the message of God's love and to make each person know they are a part of His work. Some people are good business people. Some are great musicians. Some can write. Some are gifted in praying ... everyone is different. But, whatever your talents and gifts are, they were given to you to be used.

God will give you opportunities if you just look for them. He may not give you big, obvious opportunities – for example, if you have the talent to sing, you may not sing for multitudes, but you may sing a lullaby to a baby in your care or an old hymn to an elderly neighbor.

Look for ways to use your talents. Don't hide what God has given you.

Hide not your talents, they for use were made.
What's a sun-dial in the shade?
- Benjamin Franklin -

Sing Your Loudest!

His pleasure is not in the strength of the horse,
nor His delight in the legs of the warrior;
the Lord delights in those who fear Him,
who put their hope in His unfailing love.
- Psalm 147:10-12 -

Some wonderful music is truly just a joyful noise. There is no question that it's fun to listen to amazing, famous musicians or to watch world-class athletes compete. It's always interesting to be around people who are at the top of their game. There is often much to be learned from them.

But there is room in God's service for all people to serve – not just for those who are famous or on their way to being famous. You may not feel that you are the best at what you do, but you can be the best that you can be. God will use that. He simply wants to see your willing heart and He will bless what you do for Him.

So, sing ... sing loudly and let God bless the music!

Use what talents you possess:
the woods would be very silent if no
birds sang there except those that sang best.
- Henry Van Dyke -

No Surprises

Cast your cares on the Lord
and He will sustain you;
He will never let the righteous be shaken.
- Psalm 55:22 -

Every new day begins as a clean sheet of paper. Regardless of what happened the day before, this new one is filled with unknowns.

How do you greet each day? Do you face it with anxiety and fear because you don't know what the day holds and you know that in the end, things are out of your control? Or can you face the day with the comfort of faith in the God who controls all tomorrows?

Think about these facts ... you know He loves you. You know He has all things under His control. You know that He has a plan for your life. So, why can't you just trust Him to handle the day ahead?

Whatever stresses come with your new day; whatever problems you face, trust the God who loves you. Nothing in this day will surprise Him!

Every tomorrow has two handles.
We can take hold of it by the handle of anxiety,
or by the handle of faith.
- Anonymous -

Live What You Believe

"You are the salt of the earth. But if the salt loses its saltiness, how can it be made salty again? It is no longer good for anything, except to be thrown out and trampled underfoot."
- Matthew 5:13 -

Scripture tells us that it is not up to us to decide who has truly made a choice for Christ and who hasn't. That's between each person and God. However, there is evidence in the lives of those who truly have asked Christ into their hearts and who seek to know Him and grow in their faith. That evidence is the fact that they live according to the teachings of Scripture.

Granted, it's a process and the growth will come as they learn to know Him better and better. The obvious thing, however, is that when a person truly chooses to follow Christ, their lives will begin to reflect what it means to obey Scripture. If a person half-heartedly turns to Christ, then the evidence of living according to their beliefs will be sketchy.

How does your life look?

He does not believe who does not live according to his belief.
- Thomas Fuller -

God's Grace

*Let us then approach God's throne
of grace with confidence, so that we
may receive mercy and find grace to
help us in our time of need.*
- Hebrews 4:16 -

Grace is an integral aspect of our
Christian faith. Grace means that we are given
God's forgiveness and love even though we do
not deserve it. We are sinners with wicked hearts
who truly deserve nothing from the Creator of the
universe.

Yet, in His goodness and grace, God does
forgive us and gives us the opportunity to know
Him, live for Him and serve Him. Grace is an
amazing gift. Because of it, we can have a personal
relationship with God Almighty. We can read His
Word and apply it to our lives and we have the
privilege of serving with Him and doing His work
in the world.

Thank God for His grace that has offered you
so much. Then, offer grace to others so that they
may also know God and accept His holy grace!

*Nothing whatever pertaining to godliness and real
holiness can be accomplished without grace.*
- St. Augustine -

Being God to Your World

*His divine power has given us
everything we need for a godly life
through our knowledge of Him who
called us by His own glory and goodness.*
- 2 Peter 1:3 -

You've heard the quote about "you are to be in the world but not of the world" and perhaps you've wondered what that actually means.

The reality is that you live in the world. There isn't much you can do about that. But, you are not to live like you are a part of the world – with the world's values and priorities defining who you are.

However, being godly doesn't mean that you are divided apart from the world but being godly helps you live in a better way in the world. It helps you be an example of a godly person who is loving, kind and sacrificial.

Godliness makes you want to be a part of God's plan to make the world a better place as God Himself is more evident in it. What a privilege!

*True godliness does not turn men out of the world,
but enables them to live better in it and
excites their endeavors to mend it.*
- William Penn -

Go ... Tell ... Love

"Therefore go and make disciples of all nations, baptizing them in the name of the Father and of the Son and of the Holy Spirit, and teaching them to obey everything I have commanded you. And surely I am with you always, to the very end of the age."
- Matthew 28:19-20 -

God wants everyone in the world to have the opportunity to know Him. He wants everyone to have the chance to accept His gift of salvation. That's because He loves everyone. We know that because John 3:16 tells us that He loves the entire world.

Will God get what He wants? Will everyone accept His gift? That remains to be seen. However, whether or not everyone chooses God doesn't change the command Jesus gave His followers to go into all the world and share the message of His love.

Some people will share in their own little corner of the world, some will travel the world to places where there has never been a witness before. But, the command is the same for all of us – go ... tell ... love.

The biblical commitment to evangelism and missions is rooted in God's passionate concern to make His name known.
- Steve Fernandez -

Love Enough ...

*"For God so loved the world that He gave
His one and only Son, that whoever believes
in Him shall not perish but have eternal life."*
- John 3:16 -

Missions, on any level could not happen if sacrifice were not involved. Think about it – those believers who leave their homelands, families, friends and comforts of the life they know and travel to faraway countries, definitely do so with sacrifice.

However, each soul won to Christ by their sacrifice is truly holy fruit. The impetus for their sacrifice comes from love – God's love for all mankind and the missionaries' love for God, which is so strong that their desire to serve Him is predominant in their hearts.

What is the responsibility of those who stay home? To be a missionary where you are by sharing God's love with those in your world. Love enough to share. Love enough to pray. Love enough to give to God's work.

*Love is the root of missions;
sacrifice is the fruit of missions.*
- Roderick Davis -

Real Love

For I am convinced that neither death nor life, neither angels nor demons, neither the present nor the future, nor any powers, neither height nor depth, nor anything else in all creation, will be able to separate us from the love of God that is in Christ Jesus our Lord.
- Romans 8:38-39 -

How many times in your life have you prayed for a miracle? We all want them. We even beg for them. Non-believers get down on their knees and pray for miracles when they are frightened and concerned; even if they have never prayed a day in their lives before.

Does God answer these prayers? Yes. But not always the way we want. Sometimes He does do miracles and a sick, loved one gets well. Sometimes He doesn't and that loved one is gone.

Does a "no" answer to a prayer for a miracle mean God loves us any less? It may feel like it, but the answer is no. His love is constant and unconditional. His choices on how to answer our prayers are just that ... His choices. The answer may be no but the love is always present.

[Miracles are] the extraordinary work of God that involves His immediate and unmistakable intervention in the physical realm in a way that contravenes natural processes.
- Phil Johnson -

Reading the Bible

*It is to be with him, and he is to read it all
the days of his life so that he may learn to
revere the Lord his God and follow carefully
all the words of this law and these decrees.*
- Deuteronomy 17:19 -

You know that Scripture is important.
You know it is God's Word. You honor it and
respect it ... but do you read it?

Ouch. That's a little personal, isn't it? Maybe,
but the honest question is: If you believe that Book
on your desk is actually the words of the living,
holy, powerful, creative, loving God who wants
you to read them so that you know Him better
and so you know how to live for Him and with
Him – why aren't you reading it? There is not an
excuse grand enough to even mumble an answer
to that question.

You know God. You know the Bible is His
Word. So ... read it.

*Scripture is to be for us what it was to Him:
the unique, authoritative, and inerrant Word of God,
and not merely a human testimony to Christ.*
- James Montgomery Boice -

Good Advertising

"Let your light shine before others,
that they may see your good deeds
and glorify your Father in heaven."
- Matthew 5:16 -

The best advertising campaign makes you want to purchase a product, right? It makes it look so appealing and necessary that you yearn to have it. That's the way God's children should be showing the Christian life to the world.

Unfortunately, some believers choose to lead judgmental and sourpuss lives. They give the appearance that their lives are just one big effort to live by a bunch of rules. What's appealing about that? It isn't even realistic. God loves His children. He wants good things for them, even though we may not agree at the moment what that looks like.

Knowing God gives a deep inner joy that cannot be found anywhere else. Are you showing that to those around you? How are you advertising the Christian life these days?

God made you. He knows how you operate best.
And He knows what makes you happy.
The happiness He gives doesn't
stop when the party's over.
- John MacArthur -

Obedience Help

Trust in the Lord with all your heart
and lean not on your own understanding;
in all your ways submit to Him,
and He will make your paths straight.
- Proverbs 3:5-6 -

Once in a great while (every day) when my three-year-old grandson is instructed to do something, rather than obey he cries, "It's too hard!" Alas, sometimes for a three-year-old's mind, obedience does seem difficult.

Do you ever feel like responding to God's commands with that three-year-old mentality? "It's too hard, God! I can't do it!" Well, go ahead and tell Him that, because the response will be, "Trust Me. I'll help you." Isn't that awesome?

We're not in this life by ourselves. We have the help and strength of Almighty God helping us obey, learn and grow. So, when you feel that you do not have the strength to keep moving forward, remember you do not have to do anything on your own. Call on God for help – then trust that His strength and power are there for you!

Faith and obedience are inescapably related.
There is no saving faith in God apart
from obedience to God, and there can be
no godly obedience without godly faith.
- John MacArthur -

Other Books in the
GodMoments series

GodMoments for Women

GodMoments for Men

GodMoments for Moms